I Hear His Whisper

VOLUME 2

52 DEVOTIONS

BRIAN SIMMONS

BroadStreet
PUBLISHING

BroadStreet Publishing Group, LLC
Racine, Wisconsin, USA
BroadStreetPublishing.com

I Hear His Whisper

Encounter God's Delight in You

Stock or custom editions of BroadStreet Publishing titles may be purchased in bulk for educational, business, ministry, fundraising, or sales promotional use. For information, please e-mail info@broadstreetpublishing.com.

Cover design by Chris Garborg, garborgdesign.com
Typesetting by Katherine Lloyd, thedeskonline.com

Printed in China
16 17 18 19 20 5 4 3 2 1

Introduction

I love to be alone with Jesus in the early morning hours. Many mornings before the sun is up, I have spent time listening to the voice I have come to love. God whispers to those who seek Him. Yes, He will thunder with a mighty sound, but He will also whisper His words of love into our hearts.

This is the second compilation of the messages of love I have heard spoken into my heart. While God has spoken these words to me personally, each whisper will also have application for your life.

God is not silent. He has a voice, and you can learn to hear it for yourself. I trust these "whispers" will spark in you the desire to hear God's gentle voice for yourself.

These words are not meant to replace God's eternal, inspired Word. The Bible speaks clearly and gives us truth. I suggest you have your Bible close at hand as you read through these pages. Search the Scriptures to ensure what I present agrees with God's Word. God loves His people and longs for them to know Him and to obey His Word.

If you enjoy these whispers and don't want to wait for the next volume in this format, I regularly share other whispers at www.facebook.com/passiontranslation.

May the God of love bring you into His cloud-filled chamber as He whispers His eternal truths to you.

—Brian Simmons

"The sword of My power"

Listen to My words, child of Mine. I will guard you and protect you from all forms of evil. Your true calling in life is to be an overcomer, which means you will be challenged at times. Darkness is set against you, but I am the light that will split open the darkness and bring victory. Have I not promised to deliver you and to be your wraparound shield? Let your eyes focus on My shield of victory and not on the darkness of evil that shrouds the nations. Be filled with delight as you walk in My light. I will be the answer to the earth's evil.

Hold tightly to every promise that I have given you, beloved. Write My words upon your heart and fill your mind with My wisdom. The days ahead will be more than you expect, for both glory and shaking are upon you. The more severe the shaking of your circumstances, the clearer will be My invitation to partake of My glory. The storms are coming, My child, but they will bring forth My new wine and My new expression of grace for you.

You will overcome all things—I am with you. Place My armor on your soul and go forth to see your enemies vanquished. Wear My righteousness over your heart and

My delivering power on your mind. My good news will be your shoes, <u>My truth will keep you strong, and My sword of power will energize your every step.</u>

<u>Be faithful to Me and stand true.</u> You will be My overcoming witness to many, so take My words as your weapons today. You will not give in to the darkness and the weariness that is coming over My saints, but you will prevail, for I am the God of strength and the source of mighty power. Be strong, My overcoming one, and you will see My days of miracles.

EPHESIANS 6:10–11

Now my beloved ones, I have saved these most important truths for last: Be supernaturally infused with strength through your life-union with the Lord Jesus. Stand victorious with the force of His explosive power flowing in and through you.

Put on the full suit of armor that God wears when He goes into battle, so you will be protected as you fight against the evil strategies of the accuser!

Eph 1.19 – To know the surpassing greatness of His (God's) power toward us. God's power toward us is surpassingly great! It is knowing it and experiencing it. The equation is through the might of His strength

Have you ever felt like you were barely keeping your head above water? Take a moment to reflect about and write down what it means for God to be your wraparound shield, delivering you and protecting you along life's path.

_____

_____

_____

_____

_____

_____

_____

_____

_____

_____

_____

_____

_____

_____

_____

_____

"Your divine destiny"

I have called you to be Mine, to walk with Me. I am the one who set you apart from your mother's womb and brought you to Myself. My hand has been upon your life from the day you were born, My chosen one. Inside of your soul I have placed a calling, a voice that invites you to come closer to Me. When your heart responds to My voice, there you find your true self, your divine destiny. Never back away from this calling, My child. Others may, but you may not.

This is the day you must run with Me. I have drawn you to My side and won your heart over and over again. The sacred chamber of intimacy has become your hiding place. But today I call you to run with Me. The days are getting darker for those who do not know Me. There are many lives you will touch and many changes will come because of the light of My Son within you. So run. Run with Me where I take you—even to the higher places where you've not been before. Run. Be ready at all times to be My voice to the nations and My light to the world.

You have asked Me, "When will I find my destiny and true purpose for life?" Now is the time, says your God and

Father. You will run with Me. Even as My calling brought Abraham through the mysteries of My will, you likewise will be amazed at how I bring to pass the prophetic destiny for your life. What you see today will be changed. You have said to Me, "I will go and be who you have called me to be." This is the season where your destiny becomes clear and your purpose is unveiled. Do not be afraid of what comes, for what comes to you will be more of Me, My child.

SONG OF SONGS 6:12

Then suddenly my longings transported me.
    My divine desire brought me next to my beloved prince,
    sitting with him in his royal chariot.
    We were lifted up together!

Reflect on the idea that God is the One who reveals your destiny, setting you apart for His purposes from your mother's womb. Write down some of the ways God has called you to Himself, thus giving you a purpose and destiny.

_____

_____

_____

_____

_____

_____

_____

_____

_____

_____

_____

_____

_____

_____

_____

_____

_____

I hear His whisper...

"The place where love is born"

Bring your heart before Me. I will deepen your love. Loving others seems so difficult when you are distant and detached from My presence. When I draw near to you, My child, love is born. Everything that dilutes the power of My love disappears when I am near. Love flows from My presence and reaches to the lowest places in your life. The omnipotence of My love will conquer the fear and doubt that hides in your heart. Bring your heart closer to Me, for I will deepen your love.

The process I have taken you through is so that My love will be greater than your disappointment. Many react to the difficulties of life out of a heart filled with pain. But I promise that My love will win the day if you will turn to Me when others walk away. A great education is not enough to transfer My love into your heart. A brilliant mind will not be sufficient to carry a love that surpasses all understanding. Human logic will always leave you empty when you stand before the fire of My love.

My flame needs no fuel, nothing of humanity, for it is a self-replenishing fire. I will bring you deeper into My ways

as My fire burns up all that hinders love in and around you.
Bring your heart before Me now, My beloved. I will take you
to the place where love is born.

SONG OF SONGS 8:6–7

My passion is stronger
  than the chains of death and the grave,
  all consuming as the very flashes of fire
  from the burning heart of God.
  Place this fierce, unrelenting fire over your entire being.
Rivers of pain and persecution
  will never extinguish this flame.
  Endless floods will be unable
  to quench this raging fire that burns within you.
  Everything will be consumed.
  It will stop at nothing
  as you yield everything to this furious fire
  until it won't even seem to you like a sacrifice anymore.

When you are in the presence of God, His pure love reaches to the lowest places of your life, much like a river. List some low areas in your life where you need God's love to reach today, bringing healing and redemption. Rejoice in the fact that His love touches every area of your life.

_____

_____

_____

_____

_____

_____

_____

_____

_____

_____

_____

_____

_____

_____

_____

_____

_____

_____

"You will be amazed by what I do"

The time has come for you to ascend into a new realm, My beloved. Your old way of thinking must be abandoned and surrendered to the new life of My Spirit. My ways are not your ways. The ways of human beings are centered around power and influence, but My ways are paths of love that will mystify and bewilder even the brightest of people. The ways of the Spirit are unseen, yet they are mighty. Spirit life is power and wisdom that makes the simple wise. You will be amazed by what I will do with your life as you surrender to My ways.

Neither are My thoughts your thoughts. My Spirit is the divine intelligence that moves in the hearts of My people, bringing them to the fountain of truth. Many debate and argue, trying to prove their point. But My voice calls out to you in the silence and will teach you wisdom that cannot be given by men. The thoughts I have for you will bring you joy and comfort, for I hold you in My heart as My dearest treasure. You will not understand what I am about to do, but you will be amazed as My glory unfolds within you, giving you revelation light. You have the mind of Christ.

Do not be intimidated by those who consider them-selves to be wise, for they are fools. Those who scorn My wisdom will be seen as pretenders who must forsake their ways and enter into My sanctuary, where I will let them drink of the pure waters of truth and wisdom. Many times you have backed down from those who pretend to be wise, but now I call you to wait upon Me. I will give you the word of wisdom that you will speak.

My ways and thoughts will be understood as you yield to My Spirit, My child. I will teach you knowledge that comes from eternity, wisdom from above will enter your heart, and a deep fountain of truth will be opened up to you. You will be amazed by what I reveal to you and how I use you in the coming days. Sit with Me, listen to My voice, and let your heart be filled with My words, for I am love's pure light.

1 CORINTHIANS 3:18

Make no mistake about it, if anyone thinks he is wise by the world's standards, he will be made wiser by being a fool for God!

In what ways does your old way of thinking need to be abandoned and surrendered to the Lord's new way of thinking? Reflect on the wisdom that comes from God, and how that wisdom unfolds within you.
Be grateful that He has given you the mind of Christ.

_____

_____

_____

_____

_____

_____

_____

_____

_____

_____

_____

_____

_____

_____

_____

_____

I hear His whisper...

"I will bring a new joy"

Today I bring you living-understanding, living-wisdom, and a grace that moves with the rhythm of your breath. This gift will come with a bubbling joy. It is the mercy kiss of My Spirit. A new joy is given to you this day, beloved. Many come to Me day after day and ask for guidance. My sons and daughters, you long to be moved by the impulses of My Spirit and not by your own understanding. Listen, and you will hear My wind blowing where it wills. I will lead you in a way you have wanted to experience, the way of all My holy ones. I will guide you with My joyous eyes resting upon you. Look into My face, and the brightness of My love will make your path clear.

A new joy comes when you know I have planned for you every step you take before you were even born. Before you start to speak, I know every sentence that will come from your mouth. Before you go on a journey, I have gone before you to make your steps firm. The joy of being guided by My Spirit is the joy you will experience today.

Wait upon Me and I will show you the steps you are to take. When you turn to the right, you will hear My whisper in your heart, saying, "Yes, this is the way you are to walk." Supernatural guidance will end the pain of the past and free your heart to taste of the joys set before you. Your life will bring Me praise and show forth My glory. Your life course is planned and ready for you to say, "Yes, Lord, lead Me into greater glory."

In this season of new beginnings, My loving guidance will be your joy. I take your burdens and remove them. I take your fears and dissolve them. I take your anxiety and erase it forever. Rest in My ways and I will never disappoint you. A new joy is yours this very day.

PSALM 32:8–9

I hear the Lord saying, "I will stay close to you,
*   instructing and guiding you along the pathway for your life.*
*   I will advise you along the way,*
*   and lead you forth with my eyes as your guide.*
*   So don't make it difficult, don't be stubborn*
*   when I take you where you've not been before.*
*   Don't make me tug you and pull you along.*
*   Just come with me!"*

Reflect on how God has guided and instructed you,
even during those times you were not aware of Him.
In what ways did He give you joy along the journey?
Express gratitude that He has imparted to you a new joy
as you walk in His abundant wisdom and guidance.

_____

_____

_____

_____

_____

_____

_____

_____

_____

_____

_____

_____

_____

_____

_____

_____

_____

"Live a generous life"

I love to give good gifts to My children, gifts wrapped
with love and given in grace. My heart is filled with longings
to see My sons and daughters soar and excel. My Spirit is
freely given to all who call upon Me. My gifts are always
given without any strings attached. So I call you, My child, to
live a generous life for the whole world to see.

Give to everyone who asks you. Give to all you meet.
Give your prayers, your time, your love, and your money to
those who are in need. Hold onto nothing but My mercy, for
I will supply all of your needs through My Son. No one will
outgive Me. Give as your Father in heaven gives to you. Be
a true child of your Father and reflect My generous heart,
for I will fill you with an endless measure of My glory. My
children are those who shine as lights in the darkened world.

Have I not given to you all that you need, My child?
Have I not supplied more than your needs, even fulfilled
many of the longings that live deep within your heart? I
have promised to care for you and bring you into My eternal
glory. Even when you cross from death into the substance of
eternal life, My giving continues. I will never stop giving to

you, My child, for I am a generous God who loves to lavish His children with good gifts.

Live a life of generosity, a life of yielding your heart to My grace. Let Me stretch your faith and show you My faithfulness. Ask of Me, and I will give even the nations as your inheritance. Pray to Me, for I will give you a generous heart. I am your Father, the God of endless supply.

LUKE 6:38

"Give generously and generous gifts will be given back to you, shaken down to make room for more. Abundant gifts will pour out upon you with such an overflowing measure that it will run over the top! Your measurement of generosity becomes the measurement of your return."

Reflect on the fact that God is a God of endless supply. List some ways God has provided for you in the past as you have been faithful to give of your time, your treasure, and your talents. Thank Him for His sustaining grace as you constantly give away what He has given to you.

_____

_____

_____

_____

_____

_____

_____

_____

_____

_____

_____

_____

_____

_____

_____

_____

"You will not be broken by the world's fury"

I remind you, My child, of what I have endured to bring you to My side. I left all to have you. I chose you over comfort. I gave sacred blood to redeem you and make you My very own. Have you forgotten the sufferings I endured to overcome the world? My love has surrounded you, which is why you will not be broken by the world's fury.

I overcame so that you may overcome. You will face difficulties in this life, even as I faced the hatred of those I came to save. Nothing can defeat you when you hide in Me. The strength of My love is greater than the hatred of those who are blind. You will not be broken by this fallen world, beloved. You will be an agent of healing as you give your life to Me.

Every difficulty is heaven's invitation to trust Me more fully. Each temptation you face to fight back, to push your way forward, to insist on your own way, can be conquered with My love. I was tested in a wilderness. The darkness wanted to defeat Me, force Me to act on My own, and fight for My own way, but I was not overcome by evil.

You will not be defeated by the darkness that surrounds

you. You will not be broken by the world's fury. I have hemmed you in with My love. Those who saw Me in My sufferings were convinced I was defeated. They mocked Me and spat upon Me, the very Son of God. Yet they didn't know that My victory was not found on earth, but in My tender relationship with My Father. No matter what they did to Me, nothing could keep Me from My Father's love.

And so, My child, you are free, unbound, and unbroken by the darkness of this world. You will arise victorious. Faith in Me is the victory that overcomes the world. No one can extinguish the flame you have kindled in your heart for Me. You will share in My suffering, but you will also share in My triumph. We are one, unbroken by the world's fury. Stand true to Me and watch Me become your victory.

ROMANS 8:17–18

And since we are His true children, we qualify to share all His treasures, for indeed, we are heirs of God Himself. And since we are joined to Christ, we also inherit all that He is and all that He has. We will experience being co-glorified with Him provided that we accept His sufferings as our own.

I am convinced that any suffering we endure is nothing compared to the magnitude of glory that will soon be unveiled within us.

Every difficulty is heaven's invitation to trust God more fully. List some current difficulties in your life where you are struggling to trust God. Spend time in prayer, asking God to give you the faith to overcome those particular difficulties.

_____

_____

_____

_____

_____

_____

_____

_____

_____

_____

_____

_____

_____

_____

_____

_____

_____

_____

I hear His whisper ...

"I am your exceedingly great reward"

It is not to the great or famous that I give My reward, but to the faithful. The world will celebrate those who walk in step with the current trends, but I will celebrate those who take My hand and walk with Me surrounded by holiness. Quiet followers who cherish My Word and follow My ways—they are the ones who will see My hand of favor. Some follow Me out of duty, others follow Me out curiosity, but you, My chosen ones, follow Me out of delight. Take My hand and be faithful in all things, for I am your great reward.

Eden's pleasures are found within you. As you have chosen to take the narrow road, I will thrill you with My presence. The broad way has the laughter of the world with it, but the path of eternal pleasures will lead you into My heart. The joy I give overflows, for it is the boundless joy of My heart. I have taken notice of your faithfulness to Me. When others did their best to pull you away, you still found Me as your great reward. I rejoice with singing when I consider what you have yielded to Me. The world's riches are but trinkets when compared to My glory. The fickle applause of others will not steer you away from My heart. Be faithful, little one, and I will always be your great reward.

Have I not said that I am the rewarder of those who faithfully seek Me? There is no reward the world can give, for all is fruitless and fading away. Yet My eternal joy draws you in, welcomes you, and settles your heart. I have promised that no one will take this joy from you. Hold it fast and let it refresh you this day. Glimpses of eternity fasten your heart to Me and not to this world. Your faithfulness will be celebrated for all of eternity. It is not to fame that I have called you, but to faithful, quiet, and forever longings after Me. I am enough for you, My child. I am your exceedingly great reward.

HEBREWS 11:6

And without faith living within us it would be impossible to please God. For we come to God in faith knowing that he is real and that he rewards the faith of those who give all their passion and strength into seeking him.

In what ways have you experienced God being your exceedingly great reward? Write a prayer of thankfulness for all of the ways God has been there for you, rewarding you for faithfully seeking Him.

_____

_____

_____

_____

_____

_____

_____

_____

_____

_____

_____

_____

_____

_____

_____

_____

_____

"Are you weary, My child?"

Beloved one, I have chosen you to be Mine, to be close to Me. Have you grown weary with your journey? Take heart, for I will encourage you. I will be more than a Father to you. I have watched as you passed through this difficult season. I know that you have been drained of strength and stamina. Come closer, yet closer to Me, My beloved child. Divine power will surge into your spirit as you wait upon and yield to Me. I promise you that I will encourage you and strengthen you in My love. The rest I give you today will empower you for tomorrow.

The moments you spend with Me are truly My delight. Your quiet moments are My treasure, for it is then that I can give you My heart and share My strength with you. I will free you from anxiety and care in the calm of My presence. Are you weary? Linger with Me in the quiet place of My love. You will be amazed at the miracle of mercy that is revealed to you.

There is not one moment of your life when I am not present with you, ready to refresh your soul. I know you and I call you My own. I am the flame that will burn within, keeping your love strong and passionate toward Me. I delight to encourage My family, providing joyous moments of delight as they come before Me in intimacy. Nothing will diminish My love for you or weaken My resolve to make you stand complete in My grace on that last day.

My gift to you is encouragement. Let it flood into your being and strengthen you. I am the God of battles who has won the victory for you. When you are weak, I will make you strong. Do not fear, for your strength will be more than enough for the difficulties of today. And the secret of My strength is My endless love that is given to you. Encouragement from heaven is your portion today, filling you with hope and love. Don't be weary any longer, My child, but feast on the fountain of My hope.

ROMANS 15:13

Now may God, the inspiration and fountain of hope, fill you to overflowing with uncontainable joy and perfect peace as you trust in him. And may the power of the Holy Spirit continually surround your life with his super-abundance until you radiate with hope!

Have you been weary this week, drained of strength and stamina? Have you ever been that way in the past, but felt the power of the Holy Spirit strengthen you? Write of a time when God broke through and strengthened you when you were weary. Ask Him to do it once again.

_____

_____

_____

_____

_____

_____

_____

_____

_____

_____

_____

_____

_____

_____

_____

_____

"Come to My abundant feast"

Many times You have thought, *Lord, if only I could have been one of the disciples who walked with You. Witnessed Your miracles. Experienced Your presence as You walked the earth. I wish I could have been on the hillside when You multiplied bread and fish. If only I could have heard the words of grace and love that fell from Your lips.*

My child, do not long for former days, for I am in you and we have become one. Come to My feast this day. It is a feast of love greater than you have ever known, greater than you could have known when I walked the earth. It is a spiritual feast of two who have become one. Drink from the cup of bliss, the cup that is poured out for you.

Did I not promise that if you hear My voice and My gentle knock on the door of your heart, and open the door, I will come in and bring a feast? Come today and feast on My love. It is a wedding feast of the bride and Bridegroom. It will satisfy every longing in your heart. Come to My feast and let your heart be at peace. My divine fullness will be more than enough for you.

EPHESIANS 5:29–30

No one abuses his own body, but pampers it—serving and satisfying its needs. That's exactly what Christ, our example, does for his church! He serves and satisfies us as members of his body—his flesh and bones.

In what ways have you been feasting on the Lord?
And in what ways have you been feasting on other things?
Write a prayer to ask the Lord to help you learn to feast
on the abundance of His love for you this week.

_____

_____

_____

_____

_____

_____

_____

_____

_____

_____

_____

_____

_____

_____

_____

_____

_____

"My words bring life and strength"

This very day My words will mean more to you than the words that come from others. It is in My words that you find life and strength. When you are praised or when you are criticized, come back to Me and lay those words before Me. Only in My presence will you know truth. If I correct you, it is to transform you. And when I encourage you and display My love to you, receive it and rejoice in it, for it is your strength.

Those places in you that have yet to be perfected will only be changed when you commune with Me in sacred intimacy. People will correct you when you are wrong, but I will heal you when you fall. My words have the power to eliminate all of your fears. They have grace to erase your flaws. Listen to My words and cherish all that I say to you.

When your heart condemns you, know that condemnation doesn't come from Me, My child. I never condemn you; I am always greater than your heart. Do not seek the respect of others and thereby forget My words—it is My love you need. Soon you will see what I visualized you to be when I gave birth to you.

Come close to Me and I will come closer to you, until you see My glory and My beauty. I have walked close with you through your childhood years, even when you did not recognize Me. And now My words are sweeter as you grow older and more tender. I am your life source, and today I am the living Word within you. I call you My own.

SONG OF SONGS 4:7

Every part of you is so beautiful, my darling.
  Perfect your beauty without flaw within.

Write out the ways that the words God speaks are different from the words others speak. Ask God to make you more tender to His voice this week.

_____

_____

_____

_____

_____

_____

_____

_____

_____

_____

_____

_____

_____

_____

_____

_____

_____

_____

"I will be your satisfying feast"

There is no need for another to satisfy you, My beloved, for I am your feast. I am the one who brings you true satisfaction. This is the day I come to bring you contentment. Even in your contentment, your hunger for Me will grow. Did I not tell the woman at the well to take a satisfying drink and she would never thirst again? And yet as she drank of My love, she thirsted for more of Me. And so I give you today this feast that will make you hunger for My Word.

Nothing will satisfy you if you are not filled with Me. In My presence there is fullness of joy. Apart from Me you will find nothing but barrenness and brokenness. I will give you only what satisfies. If you seek for My Spirit, I will not give you a counterfeit. If you seek for My living bread, I will not give you poison. Fear will always pollute your soul and keep you from My feast. Come to Me with no fear. Come, and eat and drink of Me. My life is satisfaction found nowhere else.

Let My presence reign over you, My child. Like a banner of love, it will fly over your conquered heart. You will be My victory. You will be My feast and banqueting table. I will make you My contentment and My satisfaction as you continue to feast in My love and in My presence. Your enemies will neither disturb you nor distract you from My love, for under My wings you live and function and have your true identity. I am increasing your hunger for more. Take My living Word and eat. As you eat My Word, My child, it will become life and strength and pleasure to your soul.

SONG OF SONGS 6:2–3

My lover has gone down
into his garden of delight,
the place where his spices grow,
to dwell with those pure in heart.
I know we shall find him there.
He is within me—I am his garden of delight.
I have him fully and now he fully has me!

Have you ever experienced a deep hunger and thirst for God and His Word? What are three practical steps you can take this week that will create space in your life to increase your hunger and thirst for God?

_____

_____

_____

_____

_____

_____

_____

_____

_____

_____

_____

_____

_____

_____

_____

_____

_____

"I am the Father you need"

Set your heart before Me in My peace. You will find strength in My rest. Rest at My feet, and I will prepare your way and remove the obstacles that you face. Beloved, I know your need, I know how tired you have become, and I am concerned for your peace and health. I am the God of battles, but I am also the God of wind to soar.

When you are alone with Me, I take joy in bringing you into deeper streams of My love. I delight in filling you until you overflow because of the communion we share together. Have you forgotten your first love of passion toward Me? Have you allowed the demands of people to move your heart away from My invitation to come?

My people are experiencing awakening; the nations are ripe for harvest. I need My prophets to speak the trumpet sound that I release through them. If they are not set apart for Me, how can I instruct them with My mysteries? Remember that I strengthened my servant Elijah by the drying brook. Remember that I told Moses to strike a rock so My rivers would pour forth. The more difficult your days, the more mightily My power will be displayed in your life.

The secrets of My heart will enter into you as you sit with Me on the mercy seat. I am calling you to come with Me, to come away with Me into a place of rest. Even as the nations tremble and rage, I will strengthen you until you know Me as the God of wind to soar. My peace will grow sweeter as the days grow darker. Hear My invitation and see the opened door. I am the Father you need.

SONG OF SONGS 8:14

Arise, my darling!
    Come quickly, my beloved.
    Come and be the graceful gazelle with me.

Write a prayer in response to the reality
that God is the Father you need.

_____

_____

_____

_____

_____

_____

_____

_____

_____

_____

_____

_____

_____

_____

_____

_____

_____

_____

_____

"You have sought Me, My child"

You have served Me, sought for Me, and loved Me, even though you have not seen Me. Even when your environment was not the best, your love flourished and you found Me as your faithful God. I will never cease to listen to your voice and answer your cry. My eyes are fixed on you. Continue to seek Me, even in your difficult places, even though it seems like darkness is all around you, and I will be the light of life within you.

Do not forget that Daniel served Me while he was a captive in Babylon. He remained faithful to Me, even at a great cost. Those who were watching his life knew that I was the God of revelation secrets who gave him wisdom. Come to Me and I will be for you the God of revelation secrets. You will discover what those around you have never found. Many will yet say over you, "God is with him. God is with her." You will be My true witness. Many will find Me as they see how I strengthen you and uphold you in all of your ways.

I have set you in the perfect place to be My witness and to reflect My glory. I will change your circumstances as you allow Me to change your heart. Daniel did not suffer in the lions' den because of his sin, but because of his devotion to Me. So many of the difficulties you have faced are not punishment from My hand, beloved. They are because of the favor of My heart that covers you. I will promote you through your pain as you seek Me and remain faithful to My plans for you.

You have loved Me even when you felt like I was distant. You have sought Me even when your extreme circumstances pushed you into doubt. I will not forsake those who seek Me, for you will find that I am more than enough and all that you desire. Your confidence in Me is your deliverance—you need nothing else. No one else will satisfy your heart but Me. Let your eyes be bright with hope and the dawning light will come. You will see that your life's journey has been worth it. I will never push away the one who seeks Me. Come this day, closer to Me, and I will be your strength.

MATTHEW 4:16

You who spend your days shrouded in darkness
*   can now say, "We have seen a brilliant Light."*
And those who live in the dark shadow land of death
*   can now say, "The Dawning Light has come."*

What difficulties have you gone through in the past
that were not punishment from God, but rather His favor
covering you? Write down a couple of those difficulties.
Pray that God would be your strength
through all of life's difficulties.

_____

_____

_____

_____

_____

_____

_____

_____

_____

_____

_____

_____

_____

_____

_____

_____

"I am the One who leads you"

I have My hand upon you. I will not fail to guide you into the perfect path I have chosen. Many are the doors I have opened for you. I am your Father who watches over every part of you and every step that you take. When shadows linger on your path, I will be there to brighten your way. When you are confused, I will make My ways even more clear to you.

When your life is in My hands, you will never need to worry about what direction to go. It is not a game of hide-and-seek, searching for My will as though you had lost it. My choices for your life will prevail and you will one day see how perfectly I have guided you. I have chosen you. Because you are Mine, I have commanded My angels to be in charge of your ways. As you walk with Me, they protect and hold you so you will not stumble.

Never doubt My plans for your life, My child. I have made no mistake. You are always in My hands as the one I love. There may have been an earthly father who has forgotten his child, but I will never forget you. The blood of My Son has made you fully Mine. I have called every star by name, I have measured out the oceans of the earth in the span of My hand, and I have held the mountains of the earth and unrolled the tapestry of the skies—I will never forget you or fail to hold you near.

Watch as My mysterious ways open up before your very eyes. Many have seen My miracles and never learned My mysteries. Miracles and mysteries will be revealed as you keep your heart before Me. My dear child, I am a Father who will never fail you. I will instruct you in the way you should go. You will hear the voice of My Spirit giving you the secrets of My ways. Come closer to Me. For by My side I will whisper the words of life that will make you strong and pure for what is to come. I am the One who leads you. I will never fail you.

PSALM 25:5

Escort me along the way, take me by the hand and teach me,
*   for you are the God of my increasing salvation;*
*   I have wrapped my heart into yours.*

Hear His whisper that He is the one who leads you
through all of life. Write a prayer of surrender to
Him today, trusting that He is leading and
guiding each and every step you take.

_____

_____

_____

_____

_____

_____

_____

_____

_____

_____

_____

_____

_____

_____

_____

_____

_____

"I am your identity"

I am the One who has formed you and defined you. Others gaze on your weakness and faults, but I gaze on your beauty. Twice I have perfected you—once in your mother's womb and once when you came to know Me. You are twice purified in My eyes, for you are Mine.

Your difficulties have shaped you, but they will not define you. By creation and by redemption, you are Mine! I have set My seal over your heart and now I display you to the world as My very own masterpiece of love. I have placed My glory over your life and called you, "My radiant one!"

When you surrender to Me, it is not you who guides your life, but I am the Good Shepherd who leads you. I have served you My grace even as you have yielded to Me your heart. As you pray, your voice is sweet and your face is lovely in My eyes. Never hesitate to give Me the desires of your heart. I will bring them to pass.

The strength to endure trials and pressure flows from My life within you. Do not say, "I can't handle this test," but instead say, "I can do all things in the strength of the One who lives in me." When you speak out of your identity in Me, the surging power of My Spirit will lift you high.

I am your True Identity, My beloved. Find your pleasure in Me. The more you delight your heart in Me, the freer I become to unleash My glory in your situation. Others will find your flaws, but I have found your virtue. You trusted Me when you had nothing and no one to support you. Never doubt the burning love that I have placed within your soul. In that flame you will find Me and you will hear My voice whisper to you. Beloved, I am your True Identity.

SONG OF SONGS 1:5

The Shulamite

> *Jerusalem maidens, in this twilight darkness*
>> *I know I am so unworthy—so in need.*

The Shepherd-King

> *Yet you are so lovely!*

The Shulamite

> *I feel as dark and dry as the desert tents*
>> *of the wandering nomads.*

The Shepherd-King

> *Yet you are so lovely—*
>> *like the fine linen tapestry hanging in the Holy Place.*

Do you believe God has formed and defined your true identity in Him? Write down some ways your God-given identity gives shape to your daily life (i.e., how does your identity shape your daily behavior?).

_____

_____

_____

_____

_____

_____

_____

_____

_____

_____

_____

_____

_____

_____

_____

I hear His whisper...

"The seasons of time have changed"

Eternity is now flooding into time. This season will be the most productive and powerful season you have ever witnessed, for I am hastening My word to bring it to pass. Long-dormant promises will now spring to life as I bring you through the most rapid changes you have ever experienced.

I am the God who provides all that is needed and supplies all that you lack. Never be held back by what you call lack or need, for I call it "miracles of trust." As you trust Me, My child, I will open up doors of blessing and miraculous supply that you have never even considered before. Remain faithful to Me, for I will show you My faithful and miraculous supply. There will be no limit of resources to see My harvest of the nations reached and My bride made radiant.

This season of change will move you from passivity into passion. The fire of My love will motivate you to make sacrifices of time and treasure that you have never entered into before. I am moving upon your heart to yield to Me, to go where I send you and to do what I called you to do. Even at great personal cost, you will see Me as the great Provider and the great Promise Keeper.

The changes that are upon you will demand that you trust Me more. For in the stretching of faith, you will find Me as never before. Leap for joy, for in that leap of faith you will find My supernatural presence. Get ready for the kingdom of joy to come, even as dark shadows linger in your circumstances. Faith rejoices and will subdue doubts and fears. Watch new miracles flow through the seasons of joy that I bring.

Always be ready to open your mouth and share your living faith with those who are near. Speak forth your praises, give your bold and courageous testimony, and watch Me melt the hearts of men and women before you. A great harvest is now here. Not someday, but now—this very day! Tell them today that they can come and be with Me in paradise.

MATTHEW 28:18–20

Then Jesus came close to them and said, "All the authority of the universe has been given to me. Now go in my authority and make disciples of all nations, baptizing them in the name of the Father, the Son, and the Holy Spirit. And teach them to faithfully follow all that I have commanded you. And never forget that I AM with you every day, even to the completion of this age."

Who are some of the people you have been praying for to encounter Jesus? Write down their names and thank God that He is about to unlock the key of each of their hearts.

_____

_____

_____

_____

_____

_____

_____

_____

_____

_____

_____

_____

_____

_____

_____

_____

_____

_____

"The old order is quickly passing away"

The season of change you have anticipated has now come, My child. It will be your love for Me that will see you through the most difficult of times. Disruptive revelation that brings the shocking truth to the media, to the government, and to My church—disruptive revelation that overturns the tables of religious profit—will bring about My righteous ways.

New mission strategies are coming to you in dreams and through prayer. Great understanding of My mysteries are coming to those who sit with Me on My blood-sprinkled love seat. The old order is quickly passing away, and a new breed is arising. They will be known as daybreakers and dawnmakers. They belong to Me and to Me alone. As My fiery servants, they accelerate the changes I am bringing to the earth. They will bring back My ways of holiness and passionate love.

Have I not called you to love with all of your heart and all of your passion? This is the day of all, not part, My child. You will see *all* of My love and *all* of My power at the disposal of those who have sought My face with *all* of their hearts. The season of change has come, My child. You have heard it before, but know I declare it again: you will never be the same again, for I have placed My hands upon you, My church, My bride.

1 TIMOTHY 6:11–14

Timothy, you are God's man, so run from all these errors. Instead, chase after true holiness, justice, faithfulness, love, hope, and tender humility. There is a battle raging, so fight with faith for the winner's prize! Lay your hands upon eternal life, for this is your calling—celebrating in faith before the multitude of witnesses!

So now, I instruct you before the God of Resurrection Life and before Jesus, the Anointed One, who demonstrated a beautiful testimony even before Pontius Pilate, that you follow this commission faithfully with a clear conscience and without blemish until the appearing of our Lord Jesus, the Messiah.

As you seek God with all of your heart, soul, mind, and strength, you will see all of His love and power at your disposal. Write a prayer of surrender to God's ultimate will and ways—that you would be fully surrendered to Him during this season of your life.

_____

_____

_____

_____

_____

_____

_____

_____

_____

_____

_____

_____

_____

_____

_____

_____

"I call you to action"

This is the hour of receiving and possessing My promises for your future. Many will hear My promise of hope and My word of power. But hearing is no longer enough. It is time to step out and take it as your own. Be bold and courageous, until faith spills out from you. For I am the God who promised the land of Canaan to My servant Joshua. I gave him multiple promises regarding the vast and glorious land. I promised that I would make him victorious in battle. But I also required him to place his feet upon the land before it would be his.

Take My promises today and possess all that I give to you. The promises I gave to Joshua are promises that I give to you—step out in faith and put your feet upon My promises. Claim them as your own. Do not be timid or shrink back when you are surrounded by your giants, but see your giants as opportunities for My power and might to win your battles. Many see the giants and hide in fear. But I have called you to hide in Me, and then you will find courage to step into the fray and see your enemies defeated.

Your faith must grow in order for you to take the

promises I have made to you. I will fulfill every word of promise over your life as you partner with Me. Do not listen to the voices that tell you to be passive, for I have called you to exercise your faith until you are mighty in Me to do great exploits. Giants are defeated all around you as fear is defeated within you.

Never doubt My power to fulfill your destiny and make your dreams come true. I am the Father of fulfilled dreams and the God of sovereign power. Nothing can defeat My plan for your life except for your fear and passivity. Arise now, My child, and place your feet upon the promises, make them yours, see them fulfilled, and go out to conquer. I am your God, and I will never leave you or abandon you.

PROVERBS 28:1

But the innocent lovers of God, because of righteousness,
*   will have the boldness of a young, ferocious lion!*

What are some of the promises God has given to you
that have not yet come to pass? Write them down.
Rejoice in the fact that God's power is sufficient to fulfill
your destiny and make your dreams come true.

_____

_____

_____

_____

_____

_____

_____

_____

_____

_____

_____

_____

_____

_____

_____

"This is a day of might and power"

I have opened the heavens over your heart and over your home. You have access into My glory as you come before Me with a tender heart. I heard your cries, your sighs to know Me, and to see My glory in your situation. Trust Me for your family and for every need that is before you today. Have I ever failed to provide for all that you lack? Trust Me again and watch as the miracle is released.

Those who love Me trust Me. Rest in the strength of My love, and you will see more and more breakthroughs. To break open the way for you is My delight, for I have set My love upon you and will rescue you when you call out to Me.

Even as I taught My servant David how to win in battle, so I will give you keys to victory that will unlock your break-through. But come to Me in faith, for is anything impossible when I fight for you?

This is a day of might and power for all who trust in Me. There will be many who will tell you to quit or to walk away. But I whisper into your spirit, "Come closer to Me." The days of heaven on earth will now be revealed. My outpouring will be seen in the heavens and on the earth. Never fear the reports of people, for I am the God of the great reversal, and I promise that the days of many changes will result in the days of many miracles.

As the heavens open over your home, believe Me for all that you ask. There is no one I cannot touch and transform as you pray to Me. The unveiling of mysteries will be seen in the coming days as you continue to walk with Me. These are the days when I will pour out heaven on the earth and shake all that must be shaken so that you will come before Me with the purest of faith. It is the day of My might and power.

JAMES 4:6–8

But he continues to pour out more and more grace upon us. For it says,

> *God resists you when you are proud but continually pours out grace when you are humble.*

So then, surrender to God. Stand up to the Devil and resist him and he will turn and run away from you. Move your heart closer and closer to God, and he will come even closer to you.

Picture the heavens being opened up over your home. What would your home look like if God began to release His promised miracles in your life? Reflect and write down what type of home you would have.

_____

_____

_____

_____

_____

_____

_____

_____

_____

_____

_____

_____

_____

_____

_____

_____

"How can you fail when I am with you?"

You are arising in a faith in Me that you have only wished and longed for. I call you to come into the faith of God today, for when I speak it will be done. Hope must mature into greater faith, and expectation must see it accomplished. Listen to My voice and speak My Word, beloved. Hear My whisper and move your heart in faith to receive and proclaim what I have already placed within you. I long for a voice of faith to cry out for Me.

Will you move out with Me and watch your mountain move before you? The sword of Gideon was his faith in Me as I confirmed My Word before his very eyes. Will you let Me be your sword of faith? I send My servants in the strength of My promises, not in human strength. My presence goes with you, mighty one, so never fear. Are you able to stand in My strength alone, or will you look for human props to hold you up? When you doubt My power, you are left with only your flesh. Stand strong in the strength of your Lord, beloved.

When you see your limitations, you are blinded to My

promises. It is then that you allow the fear of failure to cripple you and prevent you from moving out with Me. It is time to fasten your heart to Mine and move forward with My Word as your strength. Flames meant to destroy you are quenched by faith. Voices of accusation meant to weaken you are silenced by My whisper. Faith becomes your shield of certain victory.

True faith is never in a hurry. It trusts wholly in Me and in My wisdom. Many trust in my power, but few wait to trust in My wisdom. I have a time and a plan that is beyond you. Trust in My power and in My wisdom, and you will never stumble or be disappointed. How can you ever fail when I am with you?

ACTS 4:29–31

"So now, Lord, listen to their threats to harm us and empower us, as your servants, to speak the word of God freely and coura-geously. Stretch out your hand of power through us to heal, and to move in signs and wonders by the name of your holy Son, Jesus!"

At that moment the earth shook beneath them, causing the building they were in to tremble. Each one of them was filled with the Holy Spirit, and they proclaimed the word of God with unrestrained boldness.

Quietly listen for God's whisper this week,
letting it silence all other voices in your life.
Write a prayer of calm, asking God to increase your faith,
which is your shield of certain victory.

_____

_____

_____

_____

_____

_____

_____

_____

_____

_____

_____

_____

_____

_____

_____

_____

_____

"You reign with Me"

What a wonderful hope I have given to you, My beloved. My work in your heart is not yet finished, although you have all of Me for all that you lack. A special and glorious work is being done in your heart, for you are My chosen and My redeemed one. My perfect work is being accomplished in your soul. The power of My blood at My altar of love will complete you in every way. Then you will be like Me and reign at My side, My eternal friend.

The victory of My cross always lives within you. Many see the pain and suffering all around in this world, but your eyes will focus on the glory and joy that is set before you. Everyone who has this hope living in them will be purified as gold. Nothing can set you aside and nothing will defeat you as your eyes are locked on to Me.

The restoration of your family will be complete as I prepare you to be a healer of many. My glory is hidden from those whose eyes are filled with the things of this world, but for you I will reveal My glory as your heart remains fastened on Me. I have called you to enter into My reigning and glorious presence, to live at My side and be eternally Mine. The kingdoms of this world will soon become My kingdom, for I am the Lord of all.

Come to Me and enter into life. Be one with Me in My reigning presence and all else will vanish. What a wonderful, living hope I have birthed within you. Set this hope as a torch that burns in your heart, and you will see with your eyes the restoration of all things, My child.

COLOSSIANS 1:27

Living within you is the Christ who floods you with the expectation of glory! This mystery of Christ, embedded within us, becomes a heavenly treasure chest of hope filled with the riches of glory for his people, and God wants everyone to know it!

Fixing your eyes on Jesus causes you to live with joy and expectation, even in the midst of suffering. Write down some ways you can fix your eyes on Jesus, even with all of the suffering you see around you. Respond with a prayer of thankfulness for the promise to reign with Him.

_____

_____

_____

_____

_____

_____

_____

_____

_____

_____

_____

_____

_____

_____

_____

"Come close to Me and sit down"

To love Me with all of your heart means to bow before My glory. Many sing the songs of My glory, but when I bring the fullness of My presence to you, it requires you to bow before Me in sacred reverence. I dwell in light unapproachable, transcendent, and different from anything you have known on this earth. Search for Me and you will learn what it means to fear the Lord.

Make your heart a citadel of worship, a castle of praise, where only what is holy and pure can dwell. To love Me in My holiness is to have a wall around your garden, a wall of protection and blessing. In this place of sacred intimacy you will find no deceit of darkness and the lies that have influenced your heart. Surrounded by My glory, you will renounce the self-absorption of your life. Come closer to Me and be lost in My love. We will delight in one another, and I will help you keep your garden fruitful and pure.

Rise up and come away with Me. Live in mystery, with no full understanding of what I am doing in your life. Faith will provide the insight you need to know where I am taking you and what I am doing deep in your soul. Many still feed on the Tree of Knowledge of Good and Evil, but I will feed you from within, where the Tree of Life has been planted. The fruit of My Spirit will satisfy you. Feast on this tree that was planted by the springs of My Spirit. Do not turn away from the unknown. Be like My faithful one, Moses, who turned aside to gaze on the fire of My presence. I will draw you into secrets where dancing flames bring revelation and wisdom to your soul.

Come close to Me and sit with Me on My mercy seat, where love is enthroned. Dwell with Me in the cloud of mystery and delight in mercy. The new and life-giving way into My presence has been dedicated for you. Enter, feast, and be delighted in My love. My secrets are reserved for those who fear Me and bow in worship at My throne. This is where you will find your destiny and pleasures forevermore.

SONG OF SONGS 2:14

For you are my dove, hidden in the split-open rock.
It was I who took you and hid you up high
in the secret stairway of the sky.

Picture a wall of holiness around the garden of your heart, where nothing can get in—a wall of protection and blessing. Write down a prayer of protection, for God to protect your heart and keep impure things out, so you can stay in this place of sacred intimacy with Him.

_____

_____

_____

_____

_____

_____

_____

_____

_____

_____

_____

_____

_____

_____

_____

_____

_____

"There is nothing I will not conquer when you trust Me"

I will deal swiftly with every plan of the enemy to defeat you or to slow down your advance in My ways. There is nothing hidden from My eyes. I call you to walk with Me in light and never fear the darkness. Shadows will not harm you. Even if you were to walk through the darkest valley of despair, still I am there. The brightness of My presence will chase away every shadow and remove every fear. I am your shield. I will protect you from the fiercest foe who rises up against you.

Come closer to Me and live close to My heart, My child. I will bring you into the secret place and give you rest. Let nothing trouble you. My presence will be your peace. Lay your head upon My shoulder and rest with Me. Entwine your heart with Mine until we are one. You already are perfect in My eyes. It is the slanderer who will always wound you in your weakness. But I will strengthen you until you stand complete, wearing My robe and My armor.

I have known all about you and your struggles, and still I call you My own, My dear one. I am faithful, even when you see your weak and frail heart—I am faithful until the end.

Did I not come and wash the feet of those I love? I will wash away the sting of your past and the defilement of your life until even your former ways are forgotten.

By passing into My presence, you will enter the realm of divine love that will cast out every fear. Choose the place nearest My heart, the place of deepest love, and I will reveal My glorious secrets to you. I will cast out loneliness from your heart. I will draw you deeper into My ways. I will meet every need you have. I will be your holy friend and faithful lover. You will discover that I am enough.

Enter into My cloud-filled chamber and I will give you the wine of My love, the joy of My heart, the peace of My kingdom, and the power of My Spirit. You will become the echo of My heartbeat. Sacred union in My chamber will make you a dispenser of mercy to those who mistreat or misunderstand you. Come and sit with Me on My mercy seat, where My love is enthroned.

HEBREWS 12:28

Since we are receiving our rights to an unshakeable kingdom we should be extremely thankful and offer God the purest worship that delights his heart as we lay down our lives in absolute surrender, filled with awe.

Picture yourself in a pitch-black room. Then picture
the light of Jesus entering the room, removing every
shadow. What dark places in your life need to come into
the light today? Write a prayer of confession, asking God
to bring His light to the dark places of your life.

_____

_____

_____

_____

_____

_____

_____

_____

_____

_____

_____

_____

_____

_____

_____

_____

_____

"This is the day of joy and gratitude"

Let your praises find true expression as you come before Me with singing and joyful celebration. True worship is the highest and most sublime form of gratitude, because in your songs of worship you are proclaiming My goodness.

When you wear the garments of praise, you are clothed in victory and breakthrough. My holy ones are robed in scented garments of praise. As you view yourself as My child, the garments of shame are taken from you and you sit enthroned with Me in robes of splendor. When you possess joy, you possess the atmosphere of glory and release it as praise. Why would you be depressed when I have brought you My greatest gift of all, the gift of My Son who brings release to every captive?

Singing praises will bring deliverance into reality. Many are the victories that have been won by praise. The overflow of grace in your life will bring you a merry heart and a cheerful countenance. When praises rise before Me, burdens are lifted from My people.

Do not be of those who withhold their praise until they

have their way. When you praise in freedom, My beloved, My will is done in your life. All that you long for will be fulfilled. Faith praises in the dark—even My servants Paul and Silas praised Me in their prison cell until the sounds of joy shook the earth and broke open the way. Not only that, beloved, but angels are released as you praise.

This is the day to bring your joyous gratitude as your love offering to Me. I give you My peace and open before you a way into My glory, for you are the heir of My promises and the child of My joy.

PSALM 136:1–5

Let everyone thank God, for he is good, and he is easy to please!
    His tender love for us continues on forever!
Give thanks to God, our King over all gods!
    His tender love for us continues on forever!
Give thanks to the Lord over all lords!
    His tender love for us continues on forever!
Give thanks to the only miracle working God!
    His tender love for us continues on forever!
Give thanks to the Creator who made the heavens with wisdom!
    His tender love for us continues on forever!

Write out a worship song that is dear to your heart,
or make one up. Then read it (or sing it!) aloud,
as a springboard for praising God this week.

_____

_____

_____

_____

_____

_____

_____

_____

_____

_____

_____

_____

_____

_____

_____

_____

_____

_____

"My armies are set in place"

My armies are battle-ready and prepared to fight. Step out in faith and watch the miracles break forth. Have I not equipped you? All who rise against you will fall, and those who disgrace My name will be set aside. But your calling is to move forward in faith and bring defeat to the forces of darkness.

Faith is the victory that overcomes the power of this world. You walk in the steps I have chosen for you and no one can hinder. Faith opens the doors to set you in the right place at the right time. You will look for your enemies and not be able to find them, for they will be defeated.

Many are My servants who step out with small faith and I work a great work. Never measure your faith by your fears, but insist that your fears submit to your faith. Your enemies fight in vain; do not be discouraged by what can be seen with your eyes, but be filled with My faith as you set your gaze on Me. Embrace truth as your best friend. Marry wisdom, for she will be your perfect partner. Cherish My peace, and you will be kept far above the fray.

I have created a clean heart within you. The virtues of

My Spirit will be born in you. As righteousness covers your heart as a breastplate, you will find a greater strength and boldness. The time has come for you to praise Me with all of your heart, for My overcomers are arising and they will not be defeated. You will praise Me for the impossibility that I changed into victory. My armies are set in place, so begin to praise Me with all of your heart!

EPHESIANS 6:10–13

Now my beloved ones, I have saved these most important truths for last: Be supernaturally infused with strength through your life-union with the Lord Jesus. Stand victorious with the force of his explosive power flowing in and through you.
Put on the full suit of armor that God wears when he goes into battle, so that you will be protected as you fight against the evil strategies of the accuser! Your hand-to-hand combat is not with human beings, but with the highest principalities and authorities operating in rebellion under the heavenly realms. For they are a powerful class of demon-gods and evil spirits that hold this dark world in bondage. Because of this, you must wear all the armor that God provides so you're protected as you confront the slanderer, for you are destined for all things and will rise victorious.

Never measure your faith by your fears,
but insist that your fears submit to your faith. Write down
some ways that your fears can submit to your faith.
Rejoice in the fact that God has made you an overcomer.

_____

_____

_____

_____

_____

_____

_____

_____

_____

_____

_____

_____

_____

_____

_____

_____

"Grace will be your song"

Your failures cannot remove you from My heart. Your weakness only attracts My grace. Come to Me when you fail, beloved, and watch My smile of compassion wash over your soul. Faith will be strengthened within you when you throw off the voice of accusation and rest in My love.

Seek My grace in your defeat, and victory will be yours. Nothing separates you from My eternal love. Many times you have rejected yourself, but I have never rejected you. Faith in My love will slay your discouragement and remove the weapons from the hands of your enemies. Hope will give birth to joy, even when you do not see My glory. It is time for a song of endless joy to fill your lips. Sing the song of triumph when you face defeat. Laugh at the enemy and you will witness My victory break forth, for I hold it in store for the upright and for those who love Me. Sin will never have dominion over you.

My strength will overcome your weakest flaw until every part of you is filled with the energy of grace. Never let go of your passion to be holy in My eyes. I will purify you with this living hope and you will see the transformation take place in

My glory. Burn holy in My presence until faith radiates from your inner being. Come into My transforming glory and expect Me to move on your behalf. Grace will be your song, and faith will be your portion.

PSALM 46:1–3

God, you're such a safe and powerful place to hide!
   You're a proven help in time of trouble—
   more than enough and always available whenever I need you.
So we will never fear
   even if every structure of support were to crumble away.
We will not fear even when the earth quakes and shakes,
   moving mountains and casting them into the sea.
For the raging roar of stormy winds and crashing waves
   cannot erode our faith in you.

Your weaknesses only attract God's grace, no matter how you feel after failure. When you fail, come to Him and picture Him smiling as He washes over you. How does this make you feel? Write down some thoughts about how God is pleased with you, even in the midst of your weaknesses.

_____

_____

_____

_____

_____

_____

_____

_____

_____

_____

_____

_____

_____

_____

_____

_____

_____

_____

"Surrender your life and all that is important to Me"

Give to Me the burden that holds you back, My child. Untie the cords to this world and come away with Me. The heavenly realm is prepared, awaiting those who are no longer chained to this earth. Greater deliverance comes to My ascending ones, for as you enter My world all that contaminates and hinders love is removed from you. I have come into your world, now come into Mine.

The confusion that comes into your soul is because you have yet to ascend into a higher place, My hiding place, where I have placed you in the secret stairway. Heaven calls you, heaven pulls you. Exchange your thoughts for Mine and take My heart and My mind as the heavenly gift I give to you. In My realm all things are possible and nothing can defeat you. In My realm there is no striving or pushing yourself forward, only resting near the fountain of the Lamb.

Will you take My glory to be more valuable than anything you possess on this earth? Will you choose to esteem what is precious in My sight? The reality of My glory makes all else dim and seem insignificant. As I shine My light of truth upon your soul, you will know how earthbound you have been. Come into My chamber room and you will see your life as I see it, as the expression of My glory.

In My realm there is no place for a divided heart, for all has been given to Me. You will not fear the dividing of your soul and spirit with My sword of light. Glory surrounds you; My glory is your shield. Your greatest protection is to be united to Me. Nothing will harm you in My burning presence. My beloved, surrender your life's purpose to Me. All that you hold in your hands and all that distracts you, lay it down before Me. You will arise and not fall; you will ascend into My glorious flames. Come away, My true friend, and make My world your home.

SONG OF SONGS 2:14

For you are my dove, hidden in the split-open rock.
   It was I who took you and hid you up high
   in the secret stairway of the sky.
   Let me see your radiant face and hear your sweet voice.
   How beautiful your eyes of worship
   and lovely your voice in prayer.

What would it be like to see life's circumstances from God's perspective? The confusion that often surrounds you is because you have yet to ascend into God's hiding place. Write down some areas where you are experiencing confusion. Ask God to let you see those confusing places from His clear perspective.

_____

_____

_____

_____

_____

_____

_____

_____

_____

_____

_____

_____

_____

_____

_____

"I give you strength as you give Me time"

The moments that you spend with Me and listen to Me are moments filled with eternity. There is no weakness, no wavering, no doubting in My presence. This is where I energize your being. Many influences have affected your life and your thoughts, but as you come into My glory I lavish upon you what you need the most: My love and My strength. You are so easily distracted and disturbed, so you must faithfully come and be with Me.

The peace I bring to you is not comparable to the peace known on earth. It transcends your mortal life and streams to you from My river of tranquility that pours forth from My throne of grace. Peace like a river will subdue your soul and wash away the words of hopelessness and pain. Come into My river of peace and float on My promises. There you will never be disappointed. Listen to Me and peace will be your pillow on which to rest your anxious thoughts.

In My love you are able to do all things, for I strengthen you with My love. People make demands on your time and your thoughts, but I wait for you to come and draw you closer when you choose Me above your friends and family. Come as My dearest one, and I will give you grace for your dearest ones on earth, so you may show them My love.

When you give Me your time, I give you My strength. Are you feeling weak today? Then come before Me until you are bathed in power. No human being can empower you, for their weapons are puny and helpless. Trust in My strength, not in the affirmation of others. Watch Me work in your heart as you "waste" your time in My presence. I will pour you out upon the earth as My gift and My treasure, full of My love.

PSALM 27:4, 8

Here's the one thing I crave from God,
the one thing I seek above all else:
I want the privilege of living with him every moment
in his house,
finding the sweet loveliness of his face,
filled with awe, delighting in his glory and grace.
I want to live my life so close to him
that he takes pleasure in my every prayer. …
Lord, when you said to me, "Seek my face,"
my inner being responded:
I'm seeking your face with all my heart.

What would your life look like if your one aim was to live in His presence? How would your priorities be rearranged? Make a list of your top-five priorities as they are lived in the light of God's presence.

_____

_____

_____

_____

_____

_____

_____

_____

_____

_____

_____

_____

_____

_____

_____

_____

_____

_____

"I am your True Friend"

I am the True Friend you have always wanted. So many times when you called to Me, I answered and I was with you. Though you are delicate, I have made you strong. Do you remember how I set your heart on fire and gave you the grace to love Me and seek Me with your whole heart? I am your wraparound shield, your strong protector, and your True Friend.

Remember the promises that I have spoken to you. Do not let them go. I promised you life, strength, healing, and power. My words will be the armor to empower you when doubts assail you from every side. Keep coming to Me and never forget the destiny I have promised you, for your inheritance was received by faith.

Your enemy knows how to wound you. He will even come through the voices of those you love the most. Be alert to My voice, My child, for I have taught you to follow My voice and not the voice of another. Remember the countless times I directed you, even on a path you had never been on before. I never failed you and I never will fail you. Always remember that I am your True Friend.

These are the days of discovery. You will discover Me in hidden places and in previously unknown ways. My voice will comfort you and bring you peace. Remember the comfort I poured out upon you when your heart was broken and you did not know what to do. I was there in that hour to mend your broken soul and restore you to Myself. I am drawn to your weakness, My beloved, like a river is drawn to the lowest places in the valley. I will fill you with My peace to sustain you and My love to empower you. Remember this, My beloved: I am your True Friend.

PROVERBS 18:24

Some friendships don't last for long,
but there is one loving friend who is joined to your heart
closer than any other!

It is important to remember that Jesus is your True Friend. Write down some ways in which Jesus never fails you, even though other friends have failed you. Spend this week praying for a greater revelation of Jesus as your True Friend.

_____

_____

_____

_____

_____

_____

_____

_____

_____

_____

_____

_____

_____

_____

_____

_____

_____

"I have a deep and tender love for you"

I am the One who has established a covenant of love between us. Expect to see My love demonstrated for you this very day, My beloved. I have never left you on your own, even when you did not perceive My love. I have never withheld from you one thing that was the best for your good or for My glory. My love is beyond logic and discovery by your mind. It is real, even as a blanket upon you on a cold night is real.

The love covenant we have together can never be broken. My love will not fail or be diminished, even when you disappoint yourself. The strength of My love is stronger than any bond. It burns brighter than a million suns. The love with which I love you, My beloved, is the same love with which My Father has loved Me. Abide in My love.

I am your Fierce Protector. Who is it that can harm you when you are locked into My heart? I love it when you trust Me and when you lean into My heart of love. I am overjoyed when you believe in My love and expect Me to work out every difficulty you face. Your trust strengthens the love covenant between us. Delight in Me today, My child, even as I delight in you. Rest in My love, for it will never fail you. Expect to see My love demonstrated for you each and every day. My love for you is deep and it is tender. Abide in My love.

JOHN 15:9–11

"I love each of you with the same love that the Father loves me. You must continually let my love nourish your hearts. If you keep my commands, you will live in my love, just as I have kept my Father's commands, for I continually live nourished and empowered by his love. My purpose for telling you these things is so that the joy that I experience will fill your hearts with overflowing gladness!"

How does it make you feel when you hear that Jesus loves you with the same love with which the Father loves Him? How can you abide in God's great love for you? Reflect on these questions and write down your thoughts below.

_____

_____

_____

_____

_____

_____

_____

_____

_____

_____

_____

_____

_____

_____

_____

_____

_____

_____

"It is My glory to show mercy"

I long to be merciful to those who turn to Me. My grace has restored your soul and your life's portion now overflows. I desire for you to be merciful to the guilty, gracious to the unworthy, and kind to those who mistreat you. Freely you have been given these virtues, now freely give them away and watch them multiply.

To hold a grudge against another is a binding chain to your soul, preventing you from arising and coming away with Me. Forgive and watch My victory be released before your eyes. I will heal your body and your thoughts when you release forgiveness to the one who offended you. My grace is flowing and it will never be stopped. Let My grace make you stronger than your enemies and wiser than your foes. I will give you the glory of grace as you give away mercy.

I am calling home the sons and daughters who have forgotten Me. You will see a waterfall of love and mercy bring my sons and daughters from afar. They will be restored with fresh passion to seek Me and to know Me. Your delight must be in finding them and loving them back into wholeness and dignity. You will remove loneliness from their hearts.

You will see them restored. Even within your family there will be healing and grace as I recapture hearts and ignite their longings toward Me.

You will be the healer of hearts and a restorer of families as I bring you higher in My ways. Give yourself to Me, forgive all who wound you, and I will work on your behalf. You will witness My victory before your eyes.

PSALM 103:8–11

You're so kind and tenderhearted to those who don't deserve it,
and so very patient with people who fail you!
Your love is like a flooding river
overflowing its banks with kindness.
You don't look at us only to find our faults,
just so that you can hold a grudge against us.
You may discipline us for our many sins,
but never as much as we really deserve.
Nor do you get even with us for what we've done.
Higher than the highest heavens—
that's how high your tender mercy extends!
Greater than the grandeur of heaven above
is the greatness of your loyal love towering over all
who fear you and bow down before you!

God has been merciful to you, forgiving and redeeming you, even when you didn't deserve it. In light of this, how can you live with mercy toward others today— especially those who have wounded you? Write a prayer of forgiveness for a person who has caused you pain. Allow the mercy of God to bring healing to your soul.

_____

_____

_____

_____

_____

_____

_____

_____

_____

_____

_____

_____

_____

_____

"Have I not promised that nothing will separate you from My love?"

The heavens will be rolled up like a scroll and the mountains may shake and fall into the sea, but My love for you will never be shaken and will never be moved. I have held you as My treasure and have longed for you, even as you have longed for Me. A fire burns within Me, an all-consuming fire of love that will never go out. The passion I have to make you Mine can never be dimmed or fade away. Every moment I carry you. You will never have to grope in the dark to find Me.

In your difficult night season, rest in My love. Never interpret My love by how it appears, but see the depth of My love by the sacrifice of My Son. It was on Calvary that I lifted Him between heaven and earth as a sign that My love is endless. My love gave up what was most precious so I could have you. Nothing shall separate you from My love: neither pain or pressure, nor grief or disappointment. Nothing is more powerful than My love.

I have promised you that I will never leave you comfortless. Is My presence not enough? Every day the glory of My presence overshadows you, even when you do not discern it. When you thirst, I give you living water; when you hunger and crave for more, I give you living bread and My satisfying peace. When you lift up your face to Me without shame, the sunshine of My love washes you and strengthens you.

My invisible ways of love have carried you through life, so never let disappointment live within you. I am your God, the mighty lover who will never be turned aside by your weak heart. I am stirred to perfect you every time I see your weakness. Your growth is My boast, for the grace I have poured upon you will bring you into greater light and greater glory. Trust in Me and watch Me work as I demonstrate the depths of My love toward you today.

PHILIPPIANS 3:20–21

But we are a colony of heaven on earth as we cling tightly to our Life-Giver, the Lord Jesus Christ, who will transform our humble bodies and transfigure us into the identical likeness of his glorified body. And using his matchless power, he continually subdues everything to himself.

God has promised to never leave you. What are some areas where you have lost sight of God's presence? Write down some ways to remind yourself that God is always near to you, even when you don't feel Him.

_____

_____

_____

_____

_____

_____

_____

_____

_____

_____

_____

_____

_____

_____

_____

_____

"I will transform you by My love"

My love for you is vast and endless. It will open your heart to true understanding of My ways and how I work in the hearts of individuals. To love is to see with clear vision. Without love you will stumble in the dark. But selfishness dies when My love fills your heart. The tests you face are tests of love—to give freely even as you have freely received. Love will win your battle and subdue what troubles you. Even as My generous love has been given to you, now you are to give and give and give again.

As you live in My love, I will show Myself through your life and through your words. Many are those around you who need Me; love them and they will see Me. The revelation of truth can only come through love. I have not given you a spirit of fear, but the spirit of love. My holy presence will spill from your heart as you overflow with My love. Many will attempt to distract you from this treasure, but your eyes are fixed on Me and I will hold you fast in My love.

The greatest treasure you will ever receive is My love. Drink deeply from this fountain until you are lifted above every distraction and every temptation. Heaven is open to all My lovers to come and drink all that you desire. Come, My child. Be lifted up in My love until all else becomes secondary.

The demands of the world are silenced by My love—there is an endless supply to satisfy. I have promised to transform you, to change you from the inside out. Allow My love to work deeper and more thoroughly within you. The change you long for will happen before your very eyes. My love has power to subdue and to conquer what troubles you. Today I renew My promise: I will transform you by My love.

JOHN 13:1

Jesus knew that the night before Passover would be his last night on earth before leaving this world to return to the Father's side. All throughout his time with his disciples, Jesus had demonstrated a deep and tender love for them. And now he longed to show them the full measure of his love.

There are so many daily activities that compete for your heart's affection. What is one action you can implement this week to silence the demands of the world as you bask in God's love? Write a summary of how you are going to make this happen.

_____

_____

_____

_____

_____

_____

_____

_____

_____

_____

_____

_____

_____

_____

_____

_____

"Come close and listen to My secrets"

Listen to the words I speak into your being, for My words will bring life and power. I long to train you to hear My whisper and know My voice. You belong to Me, and I will speak to you. Search for My truth and ask Me for wisdom, and I will give it. I will open your mind and heart to know My secrets as you come closer to Me and sit with Me.

There is a well of life that springs from My words. No other voice can delight your soul; no other sound will move your heart. Come and be prepared in My fullness. All that is broken I will heal, for I am the God of mercy and I sit upon a throne of grace. You have only discovered a portion of My forgiveness and love—there is still much to learn as I take you deeper into My ways. As you come into My light, you will see even more of My love. I am the God who heals you, the Father of endless mercies.

Will you open your heart and listen to My voice? The sound of a stranger will not stir you, only the sound of My voice. I have many mercies ahead for those who trust Me.

Your voice, your heart, your lips, and your life need to

be surrendered to Me. Rise up and be drenched in My glory. The new has come even as the old fades away. This is the season of My splendor. The signs in the heavens and on the earth will multiply, showing you that a new day has dawned. Might and power are available to all My holy ones. Both destruction and revival are coming, a day of darkness and a day of brilliant light. Come closer to Me and you will know what I am about to do and how I will use you. My faithfulness will be your shield and protection. I will come closer to you as you draw closer to Me, beloved. Remove your fear and come, for I am your Father.

PSALM 91:1–4

When you sit enthroned under the shadow of Shaddai,
    you are hidden in the strength of God Most High.
He's the hope that holds me, and the Stronghold to shelter me,
    the only God for me, and my great Confidence.
He will rescue you from every hidden trap of the enemy,
    and he will protect you from false accusation
    and any deadly curse.
His massive arms are wrapped around you, protecting you.
    You can run under his covering of majesty and hide.
    His arms of faithfulness are a shield keeping you from harm.

God longs for you to abide in Him and know His voice.
How does God's longing for your affection make you feel?
Reflect on this and write down some ways you can
sit enthroned under the shadow of the Almighty.

_____

_____

_____

_____

_____

_____

_____

_____

_____

_____

_____

_____

_____

_____

_____

_____

_____

"I will immerse you in My presence as you come to worship Me"

There are many who are content with so little when I have so much more to give to them. Because you have longed for all that I have, you will have it all. Your desire for Me has captured My heart, beloved. And now you will see Me do more for you in this season than you ever experienced before. Because you love Me, I will pour out My heart into you and merge you into My glory.

Keep on asking, for I will keep on fulfilling every longing you have. Keep on seeking Me for the new expression of My Spirit, and you will possess My kingdom in fullness. Keep on knocking on the door that is in front of you, and it will open up and bring you into My chambers where all cry, "Glory!" I have prepared a place for you to rest, an oasis of My presence. And here in this sacred place, I will impart to you all that I am, for I am your Father.

You are an awakener of others, as they witness what I am doing in your life. Many will see and trust Me. They will be drawn into a deeper place with Me because of your surrender and your obedience to My call. Move your heart closer to Me and the shadow of My power will rest upon you. Do not be passive in this hour but passionate to pursue all that I hold in store for you. Many voices will be heard telling you to stay where you are, but come closer to Me and I will show you My majesty. I will immerse you in the realm of My glory until all that is seen in you is My splendor.

PSALM 23:5

You become my delicious feast
even when my enemies dare to fight.
You anoint me with the fragrance of your Holy Spirit;
you give me all I can drink of you until my heart overflows.

Imagine yourself in a desert and you have just run out of water. You are thirsty, and all hope of finding any water is lost. All of the sudden you see an oasis, a fresh water source in the middle of the desert. That place is prepared for you by Jesus. How does this make you feel? Write out a prayer of thanksgiving for Jesus being faithful to give you water in the midst of the desert.

_____

_____

_____

_____

_____

_____

_____

_____

_____

_____

_____

_____

_____

_____

"I am working in your life"

I am removing all that blocks My free-flowing Spirit from pouring out of your life. You will walk in Me with power in the days ahead, My child. I will baptize your life in My mighty Spirit until everything has changed within you. There will be no limit to the flow of My conquering life. You will know the greater anointing to be who I have destined you to be.

Anything that takes your eyes off of Me must be discarded. Those places in your soul where you have held on to unforgiveness will be uprooted and replaced with My compassionate love. The tug of the world on your soul will be replaced with the drawing influence of My love. Pleasing others will be replaced with a fiery passion to do My will regardless of the cost. And the temptation to do something in your own strength will be replaced with the awareness that it is only by My Spirit that your life will abound and be fulfilled.

Without saying a word, your life will speak a message of truth and grace. You will walk in a new level of My power and anointing. You will begin to live as your Father in heaven—holy, pure, and filled with faith. As you set your heart on Me and give your thoughts to Me and surrender your cares to Me, there will be a new standard of glory operating. Many will see My workings in your life and know that you have been transformed as a carrier of My presence.

Your life will demonstrate that it is not by might, nor by power, but by My Spirit. I will shake the world through a generation of men and women who have surrendered to My ways and have been filled with My Spirit wind. Bring to Me your tender heart, willing to be changed in a moment as you gaze in My twinkling eyes of love. I will be known as the God who transforms, the God who can be trusted.

COLOSSIANS 1:10–11

And because of God's unfailing purpose, this detailed plan will reign supreme through every period of time until the fulfillment of all the ages finally reaches its climax—when God makes all things new in all of heaven and earth through Jesus Christ. Through our union with Christ we too have been claimed by God as his own inheritance. Before we were even born, he gave us our destiny; that we would fulfill the plan of God who always accomplishes every purpose and plan in his heart.

List some of the things that take your eyes off of Jesus, and which must be discarded. These don't have to be evil or sinful things; they may be very good things that have just taken the place of God in your life. As you give these up, God will reawaken your desires and longings for Him.

_____

_____

_____

_____

_____

_____

_____

_____

_____

_____

_____

_____

_____

_____

_____

_____

_____

"I am the God who makes all things new"

I will renew your heart and spirit this day, to know Me as the God of heaven. My presence lives within you. Where My presence abides, there is heaven. Where I am glory is found. Living within you at this moment is the heavenly glory that I have given to My sons and daughters. Many look away to heaven and fail to embrace the eternal life that dwells within them. Everything that makes heaven real lives in you, My child.

The heavenly reality will be made clear. Soon, all that is around you will become nothing more than trinkets compared to the glory that is within you. My endless grace has opened a fountain within, pouring satisfying streams into your thoughts, your emotions, your very soul. This grace fountain will be the source of life—heavenly life—within you. Love, joy, and peace is My presence in your soul. Fill your heart with My words. Never say, "I am rich and in need of nothing."

Heavenly life is My portion that I share with you today. Have I not seated you in heavenly places and enthroned you at My right hand as an overcomer? All that I am I give to you. Receive more and drink of the water of life that flows from before My throne. Heaven's gift is yours this very day.

Let your mind be renewed and brought into a heavenly perspective. You have taken your true life and it is now hidden in My realm of glory. Set your eyes and your affections on heavenly things, and watch the healing of your heart be complete. I have a heavenly eye salve that will cause your eyes to open to the brightness of My glory. I have pure robes to place upon your inadequacy and weakness. My children come into My courts and see what I have provided for My household. As they praise Me, I open doors into greater glory.

Seek My face, forsake your habits of passivity, and stir your heart to come into the heavenly chamber. I am the God who makes you new, strong, and courageous.

PSALM 26:6–8

When I come before You, I'll come clean,
approaching Your altar with songs of thanksgiving,
singing the songs of Your mighty miracles.
Lord, I love Your home, this place of dazzling glory,
bathed in the splendor and light of Your presence!

God's endless grace has opened a fountain within you,
pouring satisfying streams into you. In what ways
do you need God to pour satisfying streams into
your thoughts, emotions, and soul today?

_____

_____

_____

_____

_____

_____

_____

_____

_____

_____

_____

_____

_____

_____

_____

_____

"I long to be more real than life itself"

My promises are more faithful and true than you have ever imagined. The power of My Word has sustained you through your life and holds you near My heart. Even now your heart beats because of My promise to you when you were conceived: "You will live." Walk upon the water of My Word and trust in My promises more than sight or human skill. My Word is your strength. I have never failed to keep every promise I have given to you. My Word is more tangible and real than anything you see with your physical eyes, for all that you see has been made by My Word. I call you to step into living by faith in My Word and let all that distracts you fade away.

Trust in Me and rest in My promises. Am I not the God of abundant supply? Do I not provide for the birds, for the animals of the field, and for every one of My sons and daughters? You are the most valuable and costly part of all My creation. Sacred blood dripped from the tree to show My love. If I have given the blood of My Son to redeem you, will I not also give you everything you need as you walk with Me?

Speak My promises over your life today. Read the words I have promised you in My Holy Book. Make them real by faith. Place your hands upon My Word, for they are tangible. Trust Me. I will not fail you, for I am your Father and Great Shepherd. Believe, My child, even when all around you is contrary, for then you will demonstrate the power of faith.

I reward everyone who comes to Me in faith—My promise completed and My presence sealed upon your life. Rise up in a new wind of faith and you will not be disappointed. Take the steps that I call you to take, believe as you hold My promises. Faith is the victory you need, and My promises are the seeds of that victory. Overcome in faith and you will see with your eyes the kingdom of heaven before you.

HEBREWS 3:12–14

So search your hearts every day, my brothers and sisters, and make sure that none of you has evil or unbelief hiding within you. For it will lead you astray, and make you unresponsive to the living God. This is the time to encourage each other to never be stubborn or hardened by sin's deceitfulness. For we are mingled with the Messiah, if we will continue unshaken in this confident assurance from the beginning until the end.

Sometimes it is easy to believe God's promises for yourself, but harder to believe them for your family. What are some ways you can believe all that God has spoken about your family, trusting that His promises will be fulfilled in your loved ones? Write out a statement of faith regarding God's promises being fulfilled in your family.

_____

_____

_____

_____

_____

_____

_____

_____

_____

_____

_____

_____

_____

_____

_____

_____

_____

"Come and learn from Me"

Learn My ways as you hear My voice. Step into your place next to Me. My child, you are seated next to Me in the realm of My glory. Filling the atmosphere where we sit are the songs that cause all to cry, "Holy, holy, holy." Take your place and live in Me. Begin to see yourself as I see you. See yourself as My radiant friend, the one I have chosen. Speak the words of adoration as you take your place at My side. Speak over your life the words that affirm your place in Me.

I give to you every heavenly truth you trust in and rest upon. Earthly blessings came to My servants of old, but now every heavenly blessing I give to you as your Father. Am I not the Father of lights? I have made you My light to the world. Light and truth will draw you nearer.

The heavenly realm is yours, beloved. The kingdom of heaven is My gift to you; bring your heart into My kingdom until you are transformed from the inside out. The kingdoms of the earth will fade and fall, but My kingdom will increase and take you from glory to glory.

Seated with Me, everything is at rest. Faith becomes the flow of life when you see yourself at My side. Miracles are nothing more than My kingdom piercing the veil and coming into the earthly realm. Faith is the currency of heaven that brings miracles. Take your place of rest and believe, for My day of power is upon you. Come and learn of Me, and I will teach you My ways and unveil My heart. Sit under mercy's fountain and live in Me, for I am your God.

EPHESIANS 1:3–6

Every spiritual blessing in the heavenly realm has already been lavished upon us as a love gift from our wonderful heavenly Father, the Father of our Lord Jesus—all because he sees us wrapped into Christ. This is why we celebrate him with all our hearts!

And he chose us to be his very own, joining us to himself even before he laid the foundation of the universe! Because of his great love, he ordained us as one with Christ from the beginning, so that we would be seen as holy in his eyes with an unstained innocence.

For it was always in his perfect plan to adopt us as his delightful children, through our union with Jesus, the Anointed One, so that his tremendous grace that cascades over us would glorify his grace—for the same love he has for his Beloved One, Jesus, he has for us. And this unfolding plan brings him great pleasure!

God has chosen you in Christ before the foundation of the world. How does being chosen in Him and being seated with Him in perfect rest shape the way you interact with this world? Do peace and rest characterize your day, or chaos and turmoil? Rejoice in every heavenly blessing God has given you today.

_____

_____

_____

_____

_____

_____

_____

_____

_____

_____

_____

_____

_____

_____

_____

_____

_____

"I watch over you at all times"

Though a flood overtakes you, I will lift you high. Though fires burn all around you, I will be your shelter. Though many voices may speak to accuse you, I will be your peace. Haven't I saved you a thousand times before? You see only one, but I see the many times I have rescued you, sheltered you, covered you, and protected you from your folly. I see the times where I have protected you when you weren't even aware that you were in danger.

Take rest in your Father's works. Take joy in your Father's love. This day I will open up your eyes to see My salvation. The day of the redeemer has come. My redeeming grace will be unveiled before you. This is the day where I will arise to redeem your life and fully restore it back to Me. From today forward My presence will be upon you in unmistakable ways. My face will lead your steps and protect you from all that may come against you. Though a raging flood threatens you, I will lift you high and you will see My glory, for the day of the redeemer has come.

I am a God who stands watch over you at all times. My eyes rest upon you, not just observing you but protecting you, keeping you in My care. I provide untold favors for you, guarding you from the temptation that is too great for you—all because I love you! When I consider you, My heart is stirred to act on your behalf. There is no need for worry or anxiety, because My hand is upon you and I will lead you with My eyes. I ask for a deeper kind of confidence that goes beyond the moment and endures for a lifetime. Trust Me, and you will never be disappointed.

PSALM 46:8–11

Everyone look!

Come and see the breathtaking wonders of our God.
For he brings both ruin and revival.
And he's the One who makes conflicts to end
throughout the earth,
breaking and burning every weapon of war.
Surrender your anxiety!
Be silent and stop your striving and you will see that I am God.
I am the God above all the nations,
and I will be exalted throughout the whole earth.
Here he stands!
The Commander!
The Mighty Lord of Angel-Armies is on our side!
The God of Jacob fights for us!

List some ways that God has saved you
(from encountering Jesus for the first time to the myriad
of ways He has rescued you since then). Spend time
thanking God for His protection, for His redeeming
grace that has been made evident in your life.

_____

_____

_____

_____

_____

_____

_____

_____

_____

_____

_____

_____

_____

_____

_____

_____

"There is not one thing that can disturb you"

My Word is full of promises for you. Every promise I make is as sure as tomorrow's sunrise. I have set all things in place to cause you to advance in My ways. Every word I speak has been refined seven times and found to be trustworthy and dependable. Rest in My promises and you will succeed. What will defeat you? Is it worry that troubles you? I call you to a life free from worry and anxious care. Live a life that is free from worry. You are not to worry about anything—not one thing.

Your relationship with Me means that I will carry every burden that weighs you down so that you can take My peace as your own. Heaven is empty of worry. The abundant love of the Father provides all, loves all, and cares for all. I am the King of peace. All who dwell with Me live in a paradise of love and grace. My love will take you through this momentary difficulty. Rest with Me in the green pastures of My peace and drink from the quiet brook of bliss. Let worry be far from you—not one thing can disturb you as you rest with Me.

Never say, "It is my nature to worry," for I have given you

a life that is carefree. Has worry brought you any blessings? I will take care of your tomorrow as I have taken care of your today. Live free, far above the cares of this world. Not one thing can penetrate My wraparound presence as I go with you. Walk in paths of peace and experience My joy as you face the future, for the King of peace walks with you.

ROMANS 5:1–5

Our faith in Jesus transfers God's righteousness to us and he now declares us flawless in his eyes. This means we can now enjoy true and lasting peace with God, all because of what our Lord Jesus, the Anointed One, has done for us. Our faith guarantees us access into this marvelous kindness that has given us a perfect relationship with God. What incredible joy bursts forth within us as we keep on celebrating our hope of experiencing God's glory!

But that's not all! Even in times of trouble we have a joyful confidence, knowing that our pressures will develop in us patient endurance. And patient endurance will refine our character, and proven character leads us back to hope. And this hope is not a disappointing fantasy, because we can now experience the endless love of God cascading into our hearts through the Holy Spirit who lives in us!

Reflect on the truth that every promise God makes is as sure as tomorrow's sunrise. How would life be different if you woke up tomorrow morning and all of God's promises were fulfilled in your life? Write down a vision statement for your future self, where all of the promises of God have been brought to pass in your life.

_____

_____

_____

_____

_____

_____

_____

_____

_____

_____

_____

_____

_____

_____

_____

_____

"I hold the plans for your life"

I have a life plan for you, a plan that was written into your life record before you were even born. It is a plan to bring you to My heart and into My fullness. I am the God who created you and formed you in your mother's womb. My gaze was set upon you before your eyes were ever opened. My plan for you will succeed and you will one day say, "Abba, you do all things well!"

My timing is perfect—I make all things beautiful in My time. What you see now is not what will be forever. There may be trouble in your family, but it will not last forever. There may be trouble around you, but it will soon disappear. I hold the plans of your life in My hands. The details of this plan unfold slowly, but My divine fingerprints rest upon them. Set your heart on My faithfulness and don't be distracted by the impossibility that limits you. I am your Father and I have plans to prosper you and make you fruitful in My vineyard.

I hold your life dear, so give it back to Me and watch Me work. As your days pass by, you will look at your life and see My perfection and how I cherished you. Moments of mystery cannot hinder the hope that lives within you. Although you do not understand what I am doing in your present, turn your eyes upon Me and know that I hold the plans of your life, plans to flood you with endless delight and perfect praise. I love you, My child, and will never allow you to be tested beyond the measure of My grace to keep you. Trust in My faithfulness. I will never disappoint you.

EPHESIANS 2:10

We have become his poetry, a re-created people that will fulfill the destiny he has given each of us, for we are joined to Jesus, the Anointed One. Even before we were born, God planned in advance our destiny and the good works we would do to fulfill it!

Do you ever feel as if your life has no purpose? The truth is that God is the One who formed you, the One who created you, giving life to you. Write out a prayer expressing your belief that God makes all things beautiful in His time.

_____

_____

_____

_____

_____

_____

_____

_____

_____

_____

_____

_____

_____

_____

_____

_____

_____

_____

"I will carry you over the finish line"

What you've been looking for is right before your eyes. You only need to become a child again. You've been robbed of your childlike faith and imagination. I am restoring your heart and removing unbelief. My voice is calling out to you, saying, "Come out and learn to experience My joy again."

Life has left you holding a bag of unbelief. But I am replacing that unbelief with faith, even the gift of faith for those who dare to believe. You will no longer walk around in chains, held captive from the abundant life I have planned for you.

Every place the sole of your foot treads you will take for the kingdom of heaven. I am raising up deliverers, a new breed of people, a generation that is full of passion and that is full of life. They will no longer be bogged down with the things of this earth, but able to ascend and soar above the problems of this world.

It is My desire to give you forward thinking and forward living. I am pushing a radical faith button within you so that you will begin to pull the future into now. The work that I begin I intend to finish, for I am watching over my word to perform it. All you have to do is align your heart with Mine.

I am strengthening you today. I know just what you need and how to give it to you. There's no need to worry, for I am your strength. You will worship and serve the Lord in spirit and in truth. All of your serving and all of your victories will come from the promptings of the Holy Spirit. You are a part of a victorious army, and I will supernaturally carry you over the finish line. I am the author and finisher of your faith.

HEBREWS 12:1–2

As for us, we have all of these great witnesses who encircle us like clouds, each affirming faith's reality. So we must let go of every wound that has pierced us and the sin we so easily fall into. Then we will be able to run life's marathon race with passion and determination, for the path has been already marked out before us.

We look away from the natural realm and we fasten our gaze onto Jesus who birthed faith within us and who leads us forward into faith's perfection. His example is this: Because his heart was focused on the joy of knowing that you would be his, he endured the agony of the cross and conquered its humiliation, and now sits exalted at the right hand of the throne of God!

Have you had circumstances that have robbed you of joy and faith? God's invitation to you is to come and learn to lean on Him once again, focusing on the author and finisher of your faith. In what areas do you need God to carry you over the finish line?

_____

_____

_____

_____

_____

_____

_____

_____

_____

_____

_____

_____

_____

_____

_____

_____

_____

"My gift to you is My endless, triumphant life"

I love to give good gifts to My children, to those who are born from above. I have treasures to bestow that the world can never give, nor can they understand their value. I give to you new life, resurrection life. From the death of My body on Calvary's cross, living virtue was given. The new life I give to you will spring up within your soul and subdue everything that competes with My love. The inexpressible joy of resurrection life is My gift to you.

The world can only see Christ dying on a cross, but I am the Christ of triumphant victory leaping from the tomb as the doe of the morning. My life was not contained in a grave, for it is the life of eternal love that can never be stopped. The grave could not hold Me, but you can. You can hold Me close and dear to your heart. This is My gift to you—My endless, triumphant life.

Many are searching for what I have already given you. Take this gift and bring it to those who are near. Let your family see that I live in you and they will glorify Me. Never fear to share this gift with those in need, those who are hurting, those who are cold and hard. For hidden behind their hard hearts is a fragile soul that must experience this treasure. Open your heart to them and share My love. Freely I have given this love to you, so now freely share it with them.

My gift to you is the glad confidence that I am living within you. As I am now, so are you in this world. Rest in this confidence and great will be your peace.

ROMANS 6:22–23

But now, as God's loving servants, you live in joyous freedom from the power of sin. So consider the benefits you now enjoy—you are brought deeper into the experience of true holiness that ends with eternal life! For sin's meager wages is death, but God's lavish gift is life eternal, found in your union with our Lord Jesus, the Anointed One.

Many are searching for the gift that God has already given to you. God's great gift to you is His eternal, endless life. Explore some ways that God's gift of life can flow through you toward others.

_____

_____

_____

_____

_____

_____

_____

_____

_____

_____

_____

_____

_____

_____

_____

_____

_____

"I am bringing you forward"

Beloved of My heart, listen to the voice of your Father. I have set My love upon you and will never forget the way you have loved Me through your difficulties. Though you face a clouded dawn, the light of love will break through the clouds and shine upon you. In this new day I give you My promise: I am bringing you forward. What has hindered you in the past will soon be forgotten as the hope of a new day is made real to you.

I will bring you into a new place where you see more clearly and love more deeply. I will make Myself known to you, and you will see how I am at work in your life. You will rejoice in what I am doing within you, for you will be one who overcomes. Your faith will arise because I am bringing you forward. The calling on your life is great, yet you have forgotten many of the promises I have made to you.

Remember what I said to you when you surrendered your heart to Me. I promised to guide you and take you forward, and you responded by saying, "I will love You and serve You for the rest of my life." Remember that promise and love Me even through what intimidates you and what burdens you. Love Me where you are and watch the miracles I will work for you. Give Me your heart, as you did in the beginning, and My grace will bring you forward until you say, "All You have done in my life is good!"

PROVERBS 4:18

The lovers of God walk on the highway of light,
    and their way shines brighter and brighter
    until they bring forth the perfect day.

Where is God calling you to move forward today?
Write a declaration of faith and believe that He will
meet you as you step out into new territory.

_____

_____

_____

_____

_____

_____

_____

_____

_____

_____

_____

_____

_____

_____

_____

_____

_____

_____

_____

I hear His whisper…

"I know the burdens you carry"

Come to Me and rest, My beloved one. I know your responsibilities are many and I know the burdens you carry are great. Call Me your shepherd and I will carry you. Call Me your friend and I will listen to your heart's cry. Call Me your redeemer and I will bring restoration to your soul.

Busying yourself with many things will bring distraction and discouragement. The expectations of others will drown out My song of grace over your life. Call Me your strength and My invisible power will be seen in your life.

Never be limited by the feelings of weakness. I know the burdens you carry, burdens of past failures and the fear of inadequacy as you ponder your future. I am here with you this very moment to be more than a companion—I will be the Lord of love and the God of every tender mercy.

I long to show you that My grace is more than enough. Rise from the place of despair and betrayal, and come to Me. Call Me your burden bearer and leave all of your burdens at My feet. You will rise up with strength and be surrounded with peace.

PSALM 23

The Lord is my Fierce Protector and my Pastor.
I always have more than enough.
He offers a resting place for me in his luxurious love.
His tracks take me to an oasis of peace, the quiet brook of bliss.
That's where he restores and revives my life.
He opens before me pathways to God's pleasure,
and leads me along in his footsteps of righteousness
so that I can bring honor to his name.
Lord, even when your path takes me through
the valley of deepest darkness,
fear will never conquer me, for you already have!
You remain close to me and lead me through it all the way.
Your authority is my strength and my peace.
The comfort of your love takes away my fear.
I'll never be lonely, for you are near.
You become my delicious feast
even when my enemies dare to fight.
You anoint me with the fragrance of your Holy Spirit;
you give me all I can drink of you until my heart overflows.
So why would I fear the future?
For I'm being pursued only by your goodness and unfailing
love. Then afterwards—when my life is through,
I'll return to your glorious presence to be forever with you!

In what ways do you feel that God is your Fierce Protector and Pastor? Read through Psalm 23, writing down some thoughts to turn into prayer as you work through this psalm.

_____

_____

_____

_____

_____

_____

_____

_____

_____

_____

_____

_____

_____

_____

_____

_____

_____

_____

_____

_____

"Humility will open the way"

My people are unique, called out from the darkness of the world to walk in My living light. Your calling is a high calling, My child, for a divine trust has been given to you. All things are yours in life and eternity. Blessings you will never be able to number have been deposited into you. Humility will open the way to discover all that I am and all that I have given to you.

Be lost in wonder. Be overwhelmed in My presence. Be tender in heart as you come before Me. I will show you things that eyes have never seen nor ears have ever heard. The revelation secrets of My kingdom, I have given to you. What wealth is yours! What glory you can taste! Come as Moses came to My burning presence and be overwhelmed in the flames of holiness. Humility unlocks the doors of understanding and brings you through the gates of wisdom. Meekness is enthroned, for a Lamb sits in the middle of the universe and governs with gentleness all that I have made. Learn of Him, be joined to Him, and humility will open the way.

I have told you I will oppose the pride of humanity. There is a day in store in which all the humble of heart will be exalted and all the prideful and arrogant will be brought low. Your calling is never to judge what I am doing, but to humbly join Me in My light of life and be one with Me. My courts are paved with love. Come. I will dwell with those who tremble at My Word. I will fill those who have made room for My glory. Let these words pierce your heart today, for humility will open the way to My presence.

MATTHEW 18:1–4

At that time the disciples came to ask Jesus, "Who is considered to be the greatest in heaven's kingdom realm?"
Jesus called a little one to his side and said to them, "Learn this well: Unless you dramatically change your way of thinking and become teachable, and learn about heaven's kingdom realm with the wide-eyed wonder of a child, you will never be able to enter in. Whoever continually humbles himself to become like this gentle child is the greatest one in heaven's kingdom realm."

When was the last time you were lost in wonder, overwhelmed by God's presence, and experienced a tender heart when you came before Him? These only come by having deep humility. Write a prayer, asking for God to give you humility to join Him in doing all He is doing in the earth today.

_____

_____

_____

_____

_____

_____

_____

_____

_____

_____

_____

_____

_____

_____

"Enter into the joy and delight of your Master"

Your mind must be clean and prepared, sharpened as a tool. Your thoughts can be filled with pain, discouragement, and shame. Or your thoughts can be filled with love, excellence, and joy. The truth is that your words reflect your thoughts. It is my desire that your mind be filled with all that is admirable, praiseworthy, and pure. For it is then that you will enter into the joy and delight of your Master.

Radiant joy is yours, for your future will be paradise and endless delight. Live with your mind fixed on all that is above, where we sit together, seated in the heavens, united in love. To complain and to fill your mind with anxious thoughts is to lose your way and enter into confusion. I have not called you to confusion but peace. Forsake every thought and every word that points to pain and heartache. Let your thoughts and your words pull you into My realm of perfect peace.

Prophesy to your heart that you will be filled with grace to move into the future with no worries. Speak words of truth to that which hinders and lay aside every anxious thought. You are called to live carefree and enter into the endless joy and delight of your Master. Come and change every complaint into joyous laughter. My love is omnipotent, and My joy will introduce you to peace. I give you the gift of joy that no one can take from you.

The healing of your heart will come through laughter and joy, like a medicine to soothe your heart from the pain of what you have experienced. The world can never give to you this reward. It is a joy that is reserved only for all My lovers to experience. Enter into the joy and delight of your Master today, and watch what I will do for you.

MATTHEW 25:21

Commending his servant, the master replied, "You have done well, and proven yourself to be my loyal and trustworthy servant. Because you have been a faithful steward to manage a small sum, now I will put you in charge of much, much more. You will experience the delight of your master, who will say to you, 'Enter into the joy of your master!'"

You are called to live carefree and enter into the endless joy and delight of the Lord. As you approach Him today, turn every complaint into joyous laughter. Spend time writing down your complaints, turning them instead into promises to be overcome.

_____

_____

_____

_____

_____

_____

_____

_____

_____

_____

_____

_____

_____

_____

_____

_____

_____

_____

"I am calling all the men back to Me"

Awaken, My men of God, awaken! The hour is late, and I need you to arise and run with Me. My glorious women are surging forward with strength, like the mighty horses that run to battle. My fearless women are ready for the battle, but I need the men to arise. Put on your weapons of righteousness and take your place in battle formation. I will thunder at the head of My army. I will bring swift victory before your eyes. No power of hell is able to hinder when I arise. Come, mighty men of God, shake off your slumber and rub the sleep from your eyes and come with Me.

I have set before you an example of manhood: my servant David. I made him a king because of his love for Me. He is an example of leadership because of his courage to run after My heart. Take strength, O David's men, for I will use you in wonderful ways in the days ahead. Let your heart be filled with courage! Let your thoughts be steadfast, fixed on Me. I will lead you, and where I lead you it is impossible for you to fail.

Sons of the living God, servants of the cross, seekers of My heart—arise!

Warriors of love, poets of praise, teachers of My truth—arise!

Sacrifice all to Me, and I will give you all of My glory. Lay aside your distractions. Take the sword and slay the giant of seeking power and a name for yourself. I give you a sound mind to hear and obey all that I say. Set your heart on Me and prepare yourself, for the greatest days of glory are ahead. I call you to active duty, not part-time commitment. My sons, follow Me into the new horizons of holiness and taste the power of the ages to come. My Spirit is upon you and My Word burns in your soul. I need you, My sons. I love you. This is your day of victory. For I am calling the men back to Me, your eternal Father.

1 TIMOTHY 6:11–12

You are God's man, so run from all these errors. Instead, chase after true holiness, justice, faithfulness, love, hope, and tender humility. There is a battle raging, so fight with faith for the winner's prize! Lay your hands upon eternal life, for this is your calling—celebrating in faith before the multitude of witnesses!

Instead of listing the sins you need to run from, list some of the positive attributes you want to have manifested in your life (e.g., instead of freedom from anxiety, pray for the positive attribute of peace).

_____

_____

_____

_____

_____

_____

_____

_____

_____

_____

_____

_____

_____

_____

_____

_____

_____

_____

"A greater passion is coming"

Give me your heart. Seek Me with a greater passion. You will find My ways and I will disclose My secrets to you. It is time for the highest praises to fill your heart. I want to hear your voice this day. I want your worship to rise before Me. Many hold back their hearts from Me—they refuse to break open their souls and let My presence flood in, allowing their praises to pour out. I have made you to carry My praises to the ends of the earth.

The dark cloud you see on the horizon is a sign of My coming. Many will point to the cloud and fear, but you will point to the cloud and praise, for you know that I came to bring joy, blessing, and righteousness. My kingdom will expand and grow as the children of the kingdom praise Me. Heaven is waiting for the echo of praise to be heard on the earth. Even as My angels find their one delight in singing My praise, so you will find your life and your true identity when your praises echo the angelic sounds. Never allow the evil around you to dim the glory within you.

I have created you for My praises. Let Me hear the sound and see your glistening face as you seek Me. Many battles can only be won when the sounds of praise erupt from within. Did I not instruct My servant Joshua to shout My praises? Did I not scatter the enemies of Israel when My people sang of My goodness and glory? Fix your eyes on heaven and gaze upon Me, for you will praise and harmonize with the angelic host.

Many who look weak and weary will soon arise with Spirit wind and soar by their praises. When you bring Me joyous praises, I will bring to you the strength divine, because My joy is your strength. Enter in and find Me as all you need, for I will give you the secrets stored up for those who fear Me and delight in Me.

PSALM 149:3–6

Break forth with dancing!
Make music and sing God's praises with the rhythm of drums!
For he enjoys his faithful lovers.
He adorns the humble with his beauty
and he loves to give them the victory.
His godly lovers triumph in the glory of God,
and their joyful praises will rise even while others sleep.
God's high and holy praises fill their mouths,
for their shouted praises are their weapons of war!

In what ways have you been striving today? Fix your gaze upon Jesus, turn your heart toward Him, and begin to worship Him. Sing or write down a song of praise to keep your heart focused on Jesus. Rejoice that He gives you victory as you turn to Him in praise.

_____

_____

_____

_____

_____

_____

_____

_____

_____

_____

_____

_____

_____

_____

_____

_____

"The highway of praise"

Dearest one, as you walk along the highway of praise, I rejoice with you. It is true that you thank My Father for Me and all that I have done for you, but I also thank My Father for you too, the love gift of My Father. You have kept My word and walked deeper in My ways, even when the light was dim and uncertainty surrounded you. I see that you long to be a doer of My Word and not just a hearer, and that you have become faithful even in that which is little as you do your tasks for Me.

Walk with Me on the highway of praise, and I will remove your unbelief. You have asked Me for greater faith. I will grant it to you, but it requires that you walk in the spirit of gratitude for all things. Faith and complaining cannot live together, My beloved. You will either have great faith and gratitude, or you will have great doubts and complaining. Choose the higher way of praise and watch as your faith increases.

The ways of My kingdom are always growing. It is a beauty that grows, a faith that grows, and a holy gratitude that grows deep within you. As you lay hold of eternal life, it will manifest with an undiminished hope. Go forward. Step closer to the eternal flame. Learn the lesson of My servants Paul and Silas, who found even in a prison cell a sanctuary of praise. Lift up your voice with no thought of the past and set your heart on the joy that is before you. Walk with Me on the highway of praise, and your prison doors will fling wide open.

PHILIPPIANS 4:8–9

So keep your thoughts continually fixed on all that is authentic and real, honorable and admirable, beautiful and respectful, pure and holy, merciful and kind. And fasten your thoughts on every glorious work of God, praising him always. Follow the example of all that we have imparted to you and the God of peace will be with you in all things.

Picture yourself driving down the highway with the Lord. What attributes would the "highway of praise" have? Write down those attributes, then spend time asking God to give them to you as you turn to Him in praise.

_____

_____

_____

_____

_____

_____

_____

_____

_____

_____

_____

_____

_____

_____

_____

_____

_____

About the Author

Dr. Brian Simmons is known as a passionate lover of God. After a dramatic conversion to Christ, Brian knew that God was calling him to go to the unreached people of the world and present the gospel of God's grace to all who would listen. With his wife, Candice, and their three children, he spent nearly eight years in the tropical rain forest of the Darien Province of Panama as a church planter, translator, and consultant. Brian was also instrumental in planting a thriving church in New England (USA), and now travels full time as a speaker and Bible teacher. He is the lead translator of The Passion Translation, a new heart-level translation that expresses God's fiery heart of love to this generation using Hebrew, Greek, and Aramaic manuscripts, merging the emotion and life-changing truth of God's Word. He has been happily married to Candice for over forty-two years and is known to boast regularly of his children and grandchildren.

For more information about the translation project or any of Brian's books, please visit: thePassionTranslation.com or StairwayMinistries.org.

The way you counsel and correct me
makes me praise you more,
for your whispers in the night give me wisdom,
showing me what to do next.

Psalm 16:7